MACAWS

Contents

Scarlet and Blue and Gold Macaws

ISBN 0-87666-975-5

Black and white photos:
Kerry V. Donnelly, 29, 34, 37, 39, 43, 44, 59, 60, 69, 92; Louis A.
Di Mare Jr., 17; Loren Spiotta, 12; Louise Van der Meid, 33, 52,
55, 77, 81; Horst Muller, 73; Harry V. Lacey, 65; Jeanne Willet,
40; Three Lions, 55
Color photos are credited individually in their captions.

Distributed in the UNITED STATES by T.F.H. Publications, Inc., 211 West
Sylvania Avenue, Neptune City, NJ 07753; in CANADA by H & L Pet Supplies
Inc., 27 Kingston Crescent, Kitchener, Ontario N2B 2T6; Rolf C. Hagen Ltd.,
3225 Sartelon Street, Montreal 382 Quebec; in ENGLAND by T.F.H. (Great
Britain) Ltd., 11 Ormside Way, Holmethorpe Industrial Estate, Redhill, Sur-
rey RH1 2PX; in AUSTRALIA AND THE SOUTH PACIFIC by Pet Imports Pty.
Ltd., Box 149, Brookvale 2100 N.S.W., Australia; in NEW ZEALAND by Ross
Haines & Son, Ltd., 18 Monmouth Street, Grey Lynn, Auckland 2 New
Zealand; in SINGAPORE AND MALAYSIA by MPH Distributors Pte., 71-77
Stamford Road, Singapore 0617; in the PHILIPPINES by Bio-Research, 5
Lippay Street, San Lorenzo Village, Makati, Rizal; in SOUTH AFRICA by
Multipet Pty. Ltd., 30 Turners Avenue, Durban 4001. Published by T.F.H.
Publications Inc., Ltd., the British Crown Colony of Hong Kong. THIS IS
THE 1983 EDITION.

MACAWS

LOREN SPIOTTA

Keepers of hyacinth macaws should replace perches frequently, because the incessant gnawing of these birds will
destroy them. Photo by Hawaiian Service Slides.

According to Robert Ridgely's survey of Central and South America, the scarlet macaw is now almost extinct in Central America. Photo by San Diego Zoo.

Acknowledgments

I would like to thank Ira S. Bauer, proprietor of the Pup Tent in Summit, New Jersey, for his kindly assistance and added information. I would also like to thank him for allowing us to photograph his beautiful blue and gold macaw "Rocky."

Special thanks must also be given to Frank and Louise Terry, of the Terry Lou Zoo in Scotch Plains, New Jersey, for allowing us to photograph their majestic macaws.

Grateful thanks are also due to Dr. Matthew M. Vriends, senior and ornithological editor of TFH Publications, for his many additional notes and his guidance and invaluable comments on the text.

This manual is dedicated with deepest gratitude to Louis A. DiMare, Jr., who truly understands my love for animals, and to my parents for their encouragement and support.

1. INTRODUCTION

The majestic macaws (pronounced ma•kaw') are the largest members of the parrot family. Though there are size differences among the approximately 30 species and subspecies, all macaws have similar characteristics: large hooked beaks, long pointed tails, exotic plumage and a bare facial area known as a cheek patch. Macaws are extremely hardy birds noted for their longevity; some have lived for more than 60 years.

The macaws have a harsh, high-pitched call that is often very irritating to the human ear. Fortunately, however, these birds don't give voice all day long. They usually screech only in the early morning or later in the evening. A bored and frustrated macaw will also scream to get attention. A contented bird is much more peaceful.

Despite their harsh natural call, the talking voice of these parrots is quite soft and encompasses a greater range of sound. Though macaws are not usually known for their talking ability, given enough attention and proper training these highly intelligent and playful creatures can develop a good vocabulary. Some talented birds have even become bilingual. However, do keep in mind that talking birds cannot comprehend what they are saying. They simply repeat what they hear. You may have been deceived by a parrot when it correctly answers a question asked of it. However, this is only a conditioned response. Most of the credit should be given to the bird's patient and devoted trainer.

Most macaws have brilliant plumage encompassing a great range of color, from the deep rich blue of the hyacinth macaw to the radiant red of the scarlet macaw. These and other popular species will be discussed in greater detail in the last chapter.

Sexing macaws is a difficult task. Males usually have larger heads and broader beaks than females. Yet, because

A hybrid scarlet *x* blue and gold. This 98-day-old bird weighed 869 grams and was owned by Mr. and Mrs. Ralph Small. The vivid colors of the underparts are brighter than on most other hybrids of these two species. Photo by Ralph Small.

The same hybrid macaw as on the previous page. The bird is only 73 days old in this picture, but it weighs 975 grams—much more than its weight at 98 days. Here, the bright colors of the underparts are more clearly visible. Photo by Ralph Small.

A tame macaw perches on the arm of Mr. Ira S. Bauer. Macaws can develop a great attachment for their owner provided they are properly cared for. Photo by: Louis A.D. Mare Jr.

there are no color variations between the sexes, positive identification is always tricky. Some bird owners buy a pair of macaws for breeding purposes and later discover, much to their surprise, that the birds are of the same sex!

Macaws love to chew--it is, in fact, one of their favorite pastimes. Chewing gives the macaw needed exercise for its powerful beak as well as hours of enjoyment. A macaw will chew anything in sight to keep its upper mandible (beak)

12

from becoming too large. Therefore, it is essential that you provide your pet with plenty of wood scraps and a strong wooden perch to fulfill its chewing needs. If your macaw has the run of the house, keep your eye on it, for it will delight in destroying your furniture. Basically, macaws are not very messy, but due to their size and chewing habits they can be a bit more troublesome than some smaller parrots.

The macaws are not for everyone. Each bird has a distinct personality; no two are alike. Some adore men, while others show a marked preference for women. Still others take a liking to children. Many macaws become very attached to their owner and shy away from strangers. It is difficult to say what type of personality your bird will develop, so be prepared for the unexpected.

Though macaws can be as loving as puppies, they can also be extremely nasty. Most vicious birds are a product of manhandling. Though unfortunate, these birds should not be brought into your home unless you have the time and knowledge to undo the damage. Even then you may never be able to transform a nasty bird into a gentle pet. I therefore strongly suggest that you do not get involved with a problem bird.

Macaws are initially expensive birds to purchase, with some of them having prices running into thousands of dollars for tame birds. Because of their large size and need for activity they must be given ample living quarters. Equally important, macaws must have plenty of human attention if they are to live contented lives in captivity. However, if you have the time and desire to provide for the needs of one of these magnificent parrots, it will undoubtedly become an exceptional pet.

This picture shows how playful macaws are and how much of a crime it would be to confine them to a cage.

A group of assorted macaws decorating their surroundings with their exquisite colors. Photo by Aaron Norman.

The coloration of the military macaw is distinctive. Photo by Paradise Park, Hawaii.

2. BUYING A MACAW
SELECTING THE RIGHT BIRD

Before you actually purchase a macaw, I'd suggest you learn as much as possible about the different species in order to decide which bird is right for you and your family. There are several factors to consider. Do you have enough room for an adequate sized cage in your home? A cage for the larger macaws should be *no less* than 37" high, 24" wide and 25" long. If you don't have enough space, or feel that you might not be able to fulfill the needs of a larger bird, you might decide to buy a dwarf macaw. These smaller versions also make wonderful pets. Are you planning to keep the bird in an aviary all year round; if so, what species can adapt to such an environment? Most macaws should be taken in during the winter months, so it would be wise to know of this before you purchase the bird. Do you have children or pets? Some macaws get along well with both, others don't. A macaw can easily injure a child with its powerful beak. Children should not be allowed to play with these birds unsupervised. Do you want a bird that will be a friend to all or one that is strictly devoted to you? Most macaws grow attached to the one who cares for it.

What type of bird can you afford? The hyacinth is a beautiful and gentle creature, but it is also rare and therefore commands a very high price. Do you want a bird that will become a devoted pet or are you only interested in a flashy centerpiece for your living room? If you answered yes to the second part of this question, perhaps you'd better reconsider

Opposite:
The author is tempting a friendly macaw with a cracker. Selecting the right bird to fit your own needs and circumstances is essential to insure that you can properly care for the bird you have chosen.

Macaws are often seen to perch on the arms and head of people with whom they are familiar. Photo by Photo Lanai, Hawaii.

Opposite:
The blue and gold macaw is capable of blushing when excited. Photo by San Diego Zoo.

buying a bird altogether. A bird, like any other pet, is a living creature. It needs a lot of love and attention in order to live a contented life in captivty. If you cannot or will not give your pet what it needs and deserves from you, it will undoubtedly become bored and frustrated. In time you will have a very destructive animal on your hands. To ignore a pet bird, especially one as active as a macaw, is the same as sentencing it to a life of futility in a cage no better than a prison. So please carefully consider your reasons for buying a bird.

The last chapter of this book deals with several types of macaws. In that chapter are discussed the behavior of each species in their native lands, their coloring and also what is known of their behavior in captivity. This should give you some basic knowledge of macaws. However, I strongly suggest you visit local zoos that have these magnificent birds. Study them carefully. Talk to the person who cares for them. Try to find out as much as possible about these birds before you decide which one is for you. Pet shops are also a good place to start. Many pet shop dealers know quite a bit about exotic birds; even if they don't, I'm sure they will direct you to someone who does. Remember, buying a macaw is a lifetime investment, therefore make your choice wisely.

SIGNS OF A HEALTHY BIRD

Because macaws are large and expensive birds, it would be unrealistic to assume that they are readily available for purchase in pet shops. Indeed, very few pet shops are able to afford a macaw on their premises. However, almost all pet shop dealers are able to purchase a macaw for a seriously interested customer.

In order to have a macaw that will grow into a fine, healthy and affectionate pet, it is advisable to purchase the bird at a young age, ideally between eight months and one year. A younger bird is even better yet, but it is unlikely that you will find one for sale that is under eight months old. A young bird will be able to adapt more readily to its new owner and surroundings, whereas an older bird already has set habits and may be difficult to train. Though it is not impossible to train an older bird, it does require a great deal more of time and patience. The age of a bird when it is captured in the wild will undoubtedly affect its disposition. Those that are bred in captivity are more accustomed to humans and will probably make better pets. So when you order a macaw from a pet shop, inquire about its background.

A pet shop dealer will do the best he or she can to select a young healthy bird for you. However, it would be worthwhile to know a few facts about macaws to make sure your selected bird is indeed young and healthy.

Age and sex in macaws are nearly impossible to determine. The plumage in both sexes is virtually the same and there are no outward discriminating sex factors. Usually the male of a species is larger than the female. A healthy male macaw may also have glossier plumage. For those of you who are interested in the blue and gold macaw, it is said that they blush when agitated. Blushing occurs in the bird's naked cheek patch and is seen more often in the male of the species. Age is equally difficult to determine. However, watch for gray scaly legs and rough eye rings. These are signs of an older bird.

Assessing a bird's health fortunately is much easier. A healthy macaw should have bright clear eyes and its breathing should be calm and steady. Loud irregular breathing is often a sign of lung or respiratory disease. If a bird is having difficulty breathing it will rock back and forth on its perch and lack interest in preening itself.

A macaw's beak should be smooth and not show any signs of unusual growth. Its feathers should be sleek and shiny, tightly aligned to its body. Broken feathers or even a frayed tail aren't that serious as they will grow back. But beware of a bird that appears listless and fluffed out on a perch. A sick macaw will hold its wings slightly away from its body and its eyes will appear small as the head and face feathers will be

The yellow-naped macaw is much less expensive than the larger macaws. Photo by Horst Mueller.

The hyacinth macaw is less social than other macaws and, in the wild, is usually seen only in pairs. Photo by A.J. Mobbs.

The red-bellied macaw is rare in captivity; it as yet has not been known to have bred in captivity. Photo by Dr. Herbert R. Axelrod.

ruffled. A bird in such a condition is probably suffering from a cold or other ailments.

As macaws are easily stricken with diarrhea (actually a symptom of another problem), be sure that the bird is not soiled around the vent and that its droppings are firm and not watery.

Though it may sound ridiculous, make sure your bird has all of its toes. Healthy feet are extremely important. If a bird is sleeping on both feet, this is another sign of some disorder, since normally a bird sleeps on one foot. Any bird that has more interest in sleep than play and hides its head in the feathers on its back is also suffering from some malady.

If you are unaccustomed to caring for ailing birds and your selected macaw appers to be ill, I would suggest you ask your dealer for another. There is no point in asking for trouble and unnecessary heartache.

COST

There are several factors that influence the cost of a macaw. Among them are size, color and previous training. An untamed bird will be a lot less expensive, as will a bird with comparatively dull plumage. A pet shop dealer will best be able to tell you about the types of macaws that are available to you and their price ranges. I strongly urge you to deal with a shop you know to be respectable, one that considers the well-being of an animal more important than anything else. By so doing you will increase your chances of obtaining a healthy bird that will entertain and delight you for a good many years to come.

3. LIVING ACCOMMODATIONS

MACAWS AS HOUSE PETS

There are a number of ways to house macaws in captivity so that they will adapt readily as well as happily to domestic life. As your new arrival will be unsure and frightened in its seemingly strange and unfamiliar surroundings, it makes sense to have its living accommodations already set up before you bring the bird into your home. Having everything prepared before hand will also help to avoid further inconvenience and confusion.

If you plan to keep your macaw as a house pet, I strongly suggest you begin by purchasing a strong wire mesh or wrought iron cage or a T-perch with a removable wire mesh cover. Either enclosure will give the bird a sense of security and the feeling that this domain is "his and his alone." Later, when the bird is tame, you can remove the cover from the T-perch if you wish.

A cage for the large macaws should be no less than 37" high, 24" wide and 25" long. A cage for a hyacinth macaw must be larger yet and made of extra-strong metal. It is imperative that the bird should have ample room to stretch its wings. Also, when sitting on its perch, its tail should not be able to touch the floor of the cage nor should its head reach the top. The perch has to be made of sturdy wood as it will have to hold up under constant chewing.

Proportions of a cage are actually more important than the volume of the enclosure. A cage with greater length in relation to its height and width is better than one with equal dimensions. Greater length allows more room for needed exercise. Aside from having enough space to spread its wings, a cage should be wide enough for the bird to hide from a disturbance coming from any direction.

Two macaws are seen inspecting a possible nesting site. Photo by Ray Hanson.

Opposite:
The bond between two scarlet macaws is usually quite deep. Photo by Aaron Norman.

IMPORTANCE OF ADEQUATE HOUSING

I cannot overstress the importance of an adequate sized cage. Though it may be expensive to purchase, a good cage is essential for the bird's well-being. If you are an apartment dweller and haven't enough space for a large cage, I implore you to reconsider buying a macaw. Or if you simply can't afford to buy such a cage, perhaps you had better select a dwarf macaw or a smaller parrot. A large macaw in an ill-fitted cage can develop numerous behavior problems. To begin with, a bird that feels cramped will try endlessly to escape. In a short time its efforts will become a ritual. Some birds perform countless figure eights. Others bow continually, while others swing their heads from side to side. It's no wonder that in no time at all these birds become psychologically disturbed.

Macaws need not only a good sized cage, but also an environment rich in stimuli in order to maintain stable mental health. They need to see, hear and play with various objects to keep themselves occupied. If denied these things, the bird will become very disturbed and resort to self-mutilation. Feather plucking is a sure sign of a disturbed bird. I have seen birds pluck themselves almost completely nude. Other birds chew on their toes, which can result in loss of a toe or even an entire foot. The saddest problem of all is that once this neurotic behavior is set in motion it is nearly impossible to stop. And yet all of this needless trouble can be avoided if you furnish your bird with a good cage and ample stimuli.

Don't be afraid to pamper your bird. Buy it as many toys as you like. A change of toys adds novelty to its life. Your pet will love you for it and you will delight in watching its antics.

Of course, after your bird is tame, you should allow it out of the cage. Most macaws become lazy when they live indoors, so you may have to encourage your pet to get added exercise. You may decide to allow your pet the freedom of one room or of the entire house. Whatever you decide to do,

An aviary under construction. Although this aviary appears adequate, it is still too small for the larger macaws. A pair of dwarf macaws will fare well enough in accommodations of this size, but breeding results will not be accomplished with larger macaws in this type of housing arrangement.

remember to keep your eye on him: a mischievous macaw may well waddle itself into trouble. Although many macaws get along well with other family pets, it's best not to force introductions or keep pets together unsupervised. I have heard accounts of macaws fighting medium sized dogs to the death, the bird being the victor. Never underestimate the power or wrath of a macaw.

Some people choose to chain their birds to a perch instead of allowing it to wander about freely. I feel that this practice is absurdly ignorant as well as inhumane. Obviously, if a bird chained to a perch is frightened, it can easily break a toe or leg in its efforts to escape from harm. Furthermore, a bird should be kept as a pet, not a prisoner.

29

A hyacinth macaw is seen demonstrating its intelligence by putting together a simple puzzle. Photo by Dr. Herbert R. Axelrod.

Opposite:
The military macaw is somewhat less expensive than other macaws. This is probably because of its less than vibrant coloring and its personality, which is not quite as desirable as those of other macaws. Photo by Dr. Herbert R. Axelrod.

Playpens

Aside from its cage, a macaw should also have a perch or playpen to allow for extra exercise. One or more playpens can be set up near the cage and connected by ladders. This will make things easier for the bird that has clipped wings. Playpens can also be placed in other areas of the house for variety, but it is important that they be supplied with food and water in case it gets to be feeding time and the bird is unable to return to its cage. Playpens or perches should be equipped with toys, bells and other objects the macaw may be interested in. The perch or perches must be made of strong, durable wood that is resilient to the macaw's persistent chewing. As with most macaw accessories, a well built playpen will probably be expensive. Yet all of this should be considered before you purchase your bird. You should not own a large macaw unless you are able to provide for its needs. Remember, a contented pet is a joy to own. I might add that your macaw will probably destroy a good deal of its toys. Try not to be dismayed as you are, after all, buying these things for his amusement.

Bathing

In the wild, macaws delight in bathing in the rain. Some even like to roll in the wet grass. The household bird doesn't have this luxury so you have to compensate for it. One way to solve the problem is to purchase a man-made spray. These sprays are well worth their price as they are not only enjoyed by the birds, but most of the sprays kill mites as well. You should spray your bird at least once a week. As a precau-

Opposite:
Lear's macaw, the "smaller brother" of the hyacinth macaw, lacks the typical blue gloss in the plumage. Because of their high price, Lear's macaws are seen mostly in zoos. Their requirements are the same as those for the hyacinth.

tionary note, before spraying your bird be sure to familiarize yourself with any instructions included with the spray. Some sprays may warn you to void getting the spray in your bird's eyes; this may well be a good measure for any spray, especially those designed to rid your bird of mites.

Aside from sprays, some macaws thoroughly enjoy a good bath. However, bathing is not innate behavior and may have to be taught. You can first try placing wet greens in the

A tame bird is much more pleasant to own than one that is confined to a perch. Lack of activity can cause disease, as nitrates can collect in the body of a bird that is confined continuously to a perch or cage. If your bird must be confined, make sure it gets sufficient exercise.

bathing dish; then each time after that add a little water to the dish. Before you know it, the bird will have a full tub and fully enjoy taking a regular bath. Some bird owners allow their pets to bathe in the kitchen sink. I would advise that you not let your bird get into this habit, especially if it enjoys a shower under the tap, for it may decide to take a bath when you are not looking and possibly burn itself under hot water or even drown if the basin is full.

Drafts & Sunshine

Your pet should live a long active life if you take note of a few precautionary measures. As a concerned macaw owner, one thing you must never do is place your bird's cage directly in front of a window. In doing so either of two things may occur: the bird will become overheated from too much direct sunlight or it will catch a cold from a draft. Because your bird is living indoors, it does not have the resistance to withstand sudden temperature changes.

If you choose to cover the bird's cage at night, do so consistently, for in time it will come to expect the added insulation provided by the cover and lose some of its natural insulation. Therefore, if the cover is forgotten the bird may catch cold as it is not thoroughly protected.

Overheating can be just as harmful as a chill. Sunshine is important in moderate doses. The best solution is to place the cage in such a way that the bird can bask in the sun's rays if it chooses to, or avoid the sunlight by stepping to another section of the cage.

Cleanliness

The importance of cleanliness in regard to a macaw's well-being can not be overstressed. Because birds are susceptible to as many diseases as humans, it is imperative that their living quarters be clean at all times. Unlike humans, birds do not recover easily once they have fallen ill, and many disorders are a result of bacterial infections that stem from dirty facilities.

Therefore, I urge you to clean your bird's cage every other

day. Scrub the perches, change the gravel and wash food and water dishes. Make sure fresh food and water are given daily. You should even disinfect the entire cage once a week. Though it would be easier to avoid these chores, your bird will surely suffer from it, so do clean consistently. You will be rewarded with a healthy and happy pet.

AVIARIES

An outdoor aviary is an excellent enclosure for a macaw to live in. If you have the space and can afford to buy or build a strong aviary, it might be the ideal solution to the housing situation. Aviaries are also the best facilities for breeding purposes.

The size of the aviary is very important. It should be at least 8 feet high, 20 feet long and 6 or 7 feet wide. These are the best dimensions for the flight space. When someone walks into this area, the bird reacts by flying over him. Therefore, the door to the aviary should be only 4 feet high so the bird won't fly over you and right out the door. A "bird lock" is an even better precautionary measure. This is a small chamber entering into the flight space. You can walk into the chamber and then lock the door behind you as you proceed to open the door to the flight space. The bird lock will hamper any escape attempts. I don't mean to imply that macaws behave like crazed bats and will constantly try to gain their freedom the moment you approach the aviary. However, macaws are extremely curious and the world beyond their enclosure may seem awfully intriguing to them, so a little prevention certainly can't hurt.

Construction

Aviaries should be constructed of strong, heavy wire mesh. Two-inch hexagonal mesh is recommended for macaws, but this wiring is spacious enough to allow rats, mice, sparrows and snakes into the aviary. Therefore, it may be necessary to enclose the large wire with smaller mesh to keep intruders out. A two-foot metal strip covering the bottom of the cage will also prevent rats, mice and snakes from coming in. Spar-

As shown here, the beak plays an important role in the bird's behavior by being used as a third foot in climbing.

rows will still be able to gain entrance if you choose not to use the second layer of wiring.

Floors

There are several types of floors that may be used for aviaries. I will discuss some of their advantages and disadvantages. An earthen floor is obviously the least expensive but in the long run may well be costly. A dirt floor is easily contaminated and can cause numerous diseases. Remember that cleanliness is just as important to the aviary bird as it is to the house pet. It is very difficult to keep an earthen floor free from bacteria, and this type of floor also allows easy access for rodents. These unwelcome pests can contaminate a bird's food, frighten breeders from their nests, eat eggs and chicks and even harm full-grown birds.

Wooden floors are equally inappropriate, as they are hard to maintain, especially when damp, though they do protect against unwelcome visitors.

By far the best floor, in my opinion, is one made out of concrete. Though it may be hard on the bird's feet, there are several benefits. Cement floors can be easily cleaned and disinfected, thereby lessening the chance of disease, and they protect against invaders. You can overcome the problem of harshness to your bird's feet by covering the floor with litter of peat or shredded sugar cane.

Shelters

Macaws should be housed in pairs or alone, therefore a shelter need not be excessively large. The shelter should be located at the end of the flight space rather than at the side or middle. The shelter should also be made of concrete, so that the macaw will not destroy it by chewing it to pieces. The concrete should be applied over a wire mesh for durability and sturdiness. The wire mesh will serve as a support for the concrete before it dries as well as for a rough form of the shelter that can be rearranged before the cement is actually mixed or cast. The shelter should be equipped with several high perches. If you plan to leave your bird or birds outdoors all year long, the shelter should be insulated and heated. The insulation should be applied in such a way as to ensure adequate protection for your bird from the elements as well as adequate protection for your bird from himself. Insulating materials can be deadly if ingested by your bird, so care should be used in selecting and applying the material to the shelter. The heating of the shelter can also result in a situation that can be dangerous to your bird. Too much heat, improper electrical fixtures or exposed wires that the macaw can chew on may prove deadly to your pet.

It would also be a good idea to cover a portion of the flight space to protect against rain and snow. The flight space as well as shelter should have several strong wooden perches.

Hand-feeding with treats is sometimes used in training macaws. Shown is Joseph Young of Jackson, N.J. coaxing a macaw down from a branch with a bit of blueberry.

I'd suggest you give your bird extra wood chips or even a 1" by 2" stick occasionally to satisfy its chewing needs.

FEEDERS AND WATER CONTAINERS

There are many types of feeders available. Open dishes are frequently used, but macaws enjoy splattering their seed around when it is given to them in open pans. A better feeder is one that has a storage capacity allowing a limited amount of food accessible to the bird. This type saves a lot of waste. Your pet store should have various feeders available for you to choose from.

The best water containers are made of crockery, pottery or glass, the materials most durable and easiest to clean. Steel and aluminum really don't make satisfactory containers, as they rust and get pitted.

• • • •

The decision on how to accommodate a macaw is strictly up to the bird owner. No matter what you decide, always keep in mind the importance of cleanliness, adequate space and sufficient stimuli. Adherence to this rule should ensure the health and well-being of your pet.

4. FEEDING

A proper diet is essential in order to ensure your macaw a long and healthy life in captivity. It is not necessary to try and duplicate the type of diet a macaw is accustomed to in the wild. In fact, to do so might even prove harmful to the pet bird.

In the wild, macaws eat a good deal of nuts, seeds from trees and many fruits, all of which are quite high in calories. Because macaws are very active in their native lands, there is a greater need for extra calories. In captivity, however, the opposite is true. Domestic birds are a lot less active and therefore have trouble burning off calories. If they are given too many rich foods, they will soon become fat and lazy. Yet, because caged macaws prefer these foods and will eat them continuously if allowed to do so, it is the owner's responsibility to make sure his pet is not overly indulged.

Macaws are like people in that they all develop individual tastes. However, the similarity ends there. Macaws are creatures of habit. They want and expect the same meal day in and day out. They are not the least bit interested in trying something new and different. In fact, they often refuse any change of diet. A special treat (a slice of apple, a dab of peanut butter) is perhaps the only exception. Macaws thrive on routine; therefore it is best to feed, water and clean at the same time each day. Any change in routine is apt to make your bird nervous and suspicious. It is also advisable to keep the same water and feed dishes for as long as possible. Though changing containers probably won't create any serious problems, it might cause your bird to go off its feed for a few days.

Opposite:
A healthy bird eating healthful food. If cared for properly, this bird could be part of the family for well more than one generation.

41

Pet macaws should have a diet that is high in protein. Sunflower seeds are a commonly used macaw food. But as they are rich in fats, if fed to your macaw exclusively the bird will become fat, its beak and claws overgrown and its plumage dull. Mineral and vitamin deficiences may also develop. Therefore it is essential that your macaw be given a well rounded diet. Such a diet would consist of a good parrot mix (preferably bagged, not boxed, as it will stay fresher), health grit, cuttlebone or lava stone, greenfood and a dietary supplement. Pumpkin seeds, raw unsalted peanuts, safflower, pigeon feed, brewers yeast pellets and a small portion of good dry kibble dog food also add to a well balanced diet.

All macaws must have gravel or health grit added to their diet, both of which serve a dual purpose. First and foremost, because birds have no teeth to chew their food, the gravel or grit helps to grind seeds up in their gizzard. Second, they furnish the bird with several important minerals that may be lacking in their other foods. Therefore it is wise to purchase a prepared grit from a pet shop. Ordinary sand or gravel is a poor substitute and may even be dangerous to your bird's health.

Cuttlebone helps to keep a bird's beak trim and it also provides needed calcium and salt. As many macaws destroy a cuttlebone just seconds after it is offered to them, some macaw owners give their pets lava stone, which is larger, tougher and serves the same purpose.

Greenfoods should be given sparingly, as they often cause diarrhea. Lettuce has little nutritional value and should not be fed to your pet. Carrot tops and dandelions are much more nutritious, as well as watercress, green peas in the pod, celery, carrots, ripe tomato and corn on the cob.

Dietary supplements consist of liquid vitamins that dissolve in water. They should be given daily.

Fruits, like greens, can cause diarrhea, but they are an acceptable food source if given in small quantities. Macaws enjoy a bit of orange, apple, banana, soaked raisins and a few grapes. They also like Brazil nuts and large dog biscuits as a special treat.

Your pet should always be provided with fresh, cool water. Water dishes should be cleaned daily to protect against infectious bacteria.

If you follow the diet as it is given here, your macaw should remain healthy and content for a good many years.

Chewing branches is an important part of the behavior of the macaw, so be sure there are always pieces of branches (willow and fruit trees) available to your bird.

5. TAMING AND TRAINING

Patience, love and understanding are the key ingredients needed to successfully tame and eventually train a macaw. Given the proper attention, a macaw can be as loving and gentle as any pet dog. By the same token, if this highly intelligent animal is mistreated or frightened during training, it can become extremely vicious. Because a macaw has a powerful beak and grasping claws, if this should happen you could very well find yourself in a dangerous situation. Though you should not feel intimidated by your pet, it is important to approach it cautiously and as confidently as possible. A bird can easily detect human fear and will then become frightened itself. A fear biter is as potentially dangerous as the vicious bird.

As previously mentioned, macaws have very distinct personalities. You may find that you have purchased a naturally nasty bird. There is a chance that you will eventually be able to gain the bird's trust, but some macaws will never become gentle. You may then have to decide if it is wise to keep the bird in your home.

Before you begin taming your macaw, it is important to remember that you must never punish your pet, for though the macaw is intelligent, it does not have the mentality to comprehend why it is being punished. In the past some bird owners would rap their parrots over the head if they

Opposite:
If you wish to keep a tame macaw loose in a yard, you should first check with your neighbors. Not everyone will appreciate the screeching sounds or the damage to fruit trees, etc. that results from the keeping of macaws.

misbehaved. Having no idea why they were being so unjustly treated, the birds became frightened and nasty. Most often if you love your bird and treat it kindly it will reciprocate in the same fashion.

Before you attempt to tame your bird, it is essential that you gain its trust. I would suggest you begin by placing the bird's cage in an area where there is a lot of human activity. The family room would be ideal. Macaws are naturally curious and will enjoy all the goings on. Approach the cage frequently, talking quietly to your bird. Sudden gestures or noises will upset your new arrival, so try to minimize distractions. In short order the bird should adapt to its human environment.

Wing Clipping

At this point I would like to discuss wing clipping. Though this procedure may seem cruel to some, it is really quite harmless. It may, in fact, spare you and your pet needless stress. If a bird escapes during the initial period of taming it can become traumatized while you attempt to recapture it. All progress you have made to this point may be lost. Recapturing a frightened macaw is no fun for you either. Even a completely tame bird might escape if frightened. Usually a macaw is perfectly content to stay within the security of its home. However, if something should alarm your bird and it flies away, it will become hopelessly lost.

Wing clipping is perfectly painless if done correctly. There are several ways of going about it. Some experts like to clip the primary flight feathers on both wings to give the bird a balanced look. Others prefer to clip all primary flight feathers on just one wing. This method is often preferred because the bird abandons all efforts to fly. When a bird tries to fly with a clipped wing it never reaches its intended goal, as it flies in a curve. After a few more attempts, the bird gets discouraged and gives up altogether.

Wings should only be clipped by those who know what they are doing. Feathers should not be cut closer than the primary coverts to allow room for a quill that might split. An ingrown feather can result from a quill that has split down into the feather follicle.

Hand Taming

Within a few days, your bird should be well enough acquainted with its new home to begin hand taming. To wait any longer than a week only wastes time and may hinder the process. Remember that careful and confident movements are essential at this time. Approach your bird slowly and quietly. Offer it some tidbit of food--a piece of apple or banana would be fine. Always talk to it reassuringly. Because you have taken away the bird's ability to fly, the only means it has left to protect itself is its beak. A young macaw will only bite if it is afraid. Remove the need for fear and you will have won half the battle.

After the bird appears to have accepted you, hold a stick (one the size of a shortened broom handle would be best) up to its chest. Most often the bird will step onto it. If it does not, a little gentle pressure just above its legs usually guarantees results. However, do not force your bird to perform. If it really objects, quit and try again later. If all is going well, the bird will grab the stick with its beak and climb onto it. You must realize that the bird is not trying to bite you; rather it is assessing the safety of this new perch by holding it firmly in its beak.

When you have gone through this routine a few times successfully, use your free hand to hold the bird's attention as you edge it over to the hand holding the perch. Once the macaw is on your hand, remove the perch. If you have done this properly, the bird probably won't realize it's on your hand if you remain calm and steady. When you feel it is safe to do so, walk around the room with the bird on your hand. It will be confused but realize that so far no harm has come to it and should remain quietly on your hand. Continue to reassure it by talking softly and offering a few more tidbits. This first session is very important. If all has gone well by

47

the time you place the bird back in its cage, future sessions should run smoothly.

In the second session you should handle the bird in basically the same fashion, only this time do away with the perch. Repeated use of a perch will result in a macaw that is totally stick trained. This is not desirable because there will always be a barrier between you and your pet. From this point forward only offer your hand or arm as a perch. In a short time the bird will probably enjoy a ride on your shoulder. By now you and your bird will have established a trusting relationship. The bird should have no reason to bite you. If it should attempt to snap at your fingers, quickly turn your wrist toward you, pulling the finger away. At the same time gently push the macaw's chin with another finger to misguide its aim. Be patient and kind and soon the nipping behavior should subside.

After a macaw is completely hand tamed it can be trained to perform endless tricks. By observing the bird's natural behavior and using a little imagination, a macaw can be taught to play with toys, ring bells and do somersaults. I had a bird that thrived on performing for me. As soon as I entered the room she'd put on a magnificent show. I was delighted with her antics, and she loved the attention she received for showing off!

Talking

Macaws are not noted for their talking ability. However, there is always an exception to the rule, and almost any macaw can learn to say a few words if you devote enough time to train it. A younger bird will become a better talker, as will a tamer bird.

The key factor in teaching a macaw to talk is "repetition." Remember, as intelligent as a macaw appears to be, it is really only a mimic. It must hear the same word over and over again in order to learn how to repeat it. Macaws can not associate spoken words with their meanings. There are several ways to teach a macaw to talk, and as long as you use one of them consistently, you should be successful.

One of the most popular methods used is a bird training record. The same word, phrase or phrases are repeated continuously. Meanwhile, you are at liberty to leave the bird and the monotony of the record's repetition. Though most of the training records on the market are devised for parakeets, they work just fine for macaws. The best records to buy have one or two simple phrases on both sides, spoken in a clear and concise feminine voice. For some reason parrots find it easier to mimic female voices than male voices, though some birds mimic both equally well. After your bird has listened to the record for awhile, you should begin repeating the words yourself. That way the bird will learn to respond to you instead of the record. The first word is always the hardest to learn, but it is usually easier after that. One drawback with this method is that you might not like the phrases selected for the record. You might in that case make a tape recording of your own voice and the words you choose the bird to learn. The principle is basically the same.

Another training method is a daily lesson routine between owner and pet. Set aside twenty minutes each day to work with your bird. Two twenty-minute sessions a day would be better but are not necessary. Choose a simple phrase and repeat it slowly over and over again. It is important that these sessions be held at the same time every day. Remember, macaws thrive on routine.

While training, some people like to cover the bird's cage to avoid distractions. This works well with some birds; others have a tendency to fall asleep. Some experts suggest having the bird perch on the trainer's hand, facing his mouth. This way the trainer has the bird's undivided attention.

It may take months before a macaw utters its first word, so be patient. Don't expect too much from your pet. After the first word has been spoken, the rest will come much easier. Once a macaw has developed a strong attachment for its human family, almost anything is possible.

6. BREEDING

Though the breeding season for macaws is in the spring, it is best to allow the prospective parents to become well acquainted before then. This process in itself may take awhile. Sometimes when a chosen cock and hen meet for the first time, they are completely taken with each other and will probably become good mates. Other pairs turn the aviary into a battleground. Don't be foolish enough to think this first encounter is merely a lovers' quarrel and will work itself out. It won't! Separate the birds immediately before one of them is injured or even killed. Other birds become neither friend or foe; they are simply indifferent. Remember that even if a pair gets along well, you may find as time goes on that they have no intentions of rearing a family. This could well be because the birds are of the same sex. Many dismayed bird fanciers have run into this very problem. In this respect, Dr. Vriends' chart may be of help.

SEXING MACAWS

HYACINTH MACAW--sexes are alike, but the hen is usually smaller.

SCARLET MACAW--sexes are alike, but female is smaller with shorter and less hooked bill.

GREEN WINGED MACAW--sexes are alike, but female has a shorter and broader bill with a more arched culmen. (The culmen is the uppermost edge of the bill).

ILLIGER'S MACAW--sexes are alike, but female has less red on the forehead (this is not always reliable, as red may vary in individual birds of either sex).

NOBLE MACAW--sexes are alike, but female somewhat smaller.

RED-BELLIED MACAW--sexes are alike, but female is smaller.

If you have several macaws, perhaps the best way to pair them is through natural selection. This is to allow the birds to choose their own mates. Place all the birds in an aviary and wait until they select partners. After this has been accomplished, keep the pairs in separate avaries, as most macaws will not appreciate company at this time.

When you are satisfied that you are working with a good pair of breeders (though you will never be completely sure of this) it is time to get them started on a good diet that will last through the breeding season. If you plan to have the birds feed their young they must have a diet consisting of various foods. Aside from the diet described in the chapter on feeding, you might add some whole wheat bread, corn on the cob, soaked grain and wheat germ oil.

Probably the most important factor in successful breeding is the size and location of the nesting box. It is a simple fact that macaws will reject the box if they aren't pleased with it. These birds like to nest on the ground in long, low boxes. The box should be at least 5 or 6 feet long, 3 or 4 feet wide and 2 feet high. Because macaws love to chew and can do considerable damage, some people choose to use a hollow tree trunk or an old barrel for the nesting box. The entrance to any of these nesting quarters should be large enough for the birds to enter and exit with ease. More than one box per pair is advisable so the birds may have a choice.

It is important that the box be securely fastened so it won't move around and alarm the occupants. The bottom should be slightly slanted toward the back to keep the eggs from rolling about. The floor should also be covered with wood shavings. These shavings should be moistened as macaws are accustomed to humidity in the wild. A dry atmosphere may harden the egg's membrane, making it difficult for the chick to peck out at hatching time.

Birds are picky about their nesting quarters. If they reject their box, try moving it to another area of the flight space. Macaws usually have a sound reason for not accepting the nesting box. It may be because they feel it is in a draft or too close to birds in another aviary. Whatever the reason, it's best to do what you can to make sure they are content.

Another consideration is the temperature in their cage. Outdoor birds may need added heat to ward off chill. A heat bulb should solve this problem.

Remember, once the hen lays her egg don't intrude on her privacy more than is necessary. Macaws are very protective during the breeding season and may be hostile toward you. Or, if they are thoroughly annoyed by human interference, they may abandon the nest. If all goes well, the hen will lay two or three shiny white eggs. The chicks will appear in 23-24 days.

Macaws usually tolerate their young for a long while after they leave the nest. However, if you choose to hand raise the baby birds, it's best to take them from their mother before they are old enough to venture out on their own.

Breeding and raising macaws is a very time-consuming project that requires a great deal of patience on your part. Try to keep this in mind when all your efforts seem to have been in vain. Successful breeding may take years, but the end result is well worth the wait.

This type of affection is part of the mating ritual.

7. DISEASES AND AILMENTS

Macaws unfortunately are susceptible to a great many disorders. No matter how hard you try to keep your pet in good health, the possibility of it becoming ill always exists. It is important to spot a disease in its early stages in order to promptly administer medication. If a disease progresses unattended, chances of recovery are very poor. As relatively little is known of macaw ailments and their cures, early diagnosis and treatment are essential.

The following is a discussion of various diseases and ailments your macaw might contract. Though I prescribe a preliminary treatment for all of them, if symptoms persist I strongly suggest you consult a veterinarian.

Colds

A macaw catches a cold in much the same way we humans do, as a result of virus infection aided by chill and draft. Unfortunately, a cold can be more serious for a bird as it might easily develop into pneumonia.

Symptoms of this disorder are typical: runny nose, sneezing, coughing, watery eyes, listlessness, lack of appetite and possibly diarrhea. The bird will probably stand with two feet on the perch, its head tucked under a wing on its back and its feathers will be puffed up. Its nostrils may become clogged with hardening discharge. In short, your bird will look and feel miserable. This condition slowly weakens the bird's resistance.

If you have other birds, it is best to isolate the sick bird as colds are contagious. You, however, are unable to catch the virus from your pet. Keep the bird in a very warm environment of at least 80-85°F. If the bird seems to be mildly infected, you can try adding a saline laxative to its drinking water for the first 24 hours. Meanwhile, wipe its nostrils with a light antiseptic every day until the discharge has cleared up. In addition, you should add 25-50 milligrams of terramycin or aureomycin to 2 ounces of water for about three or four days. If symptoms persist, you had best take your bird to a veterinarian for added treatment. Not all vets are knowledgeable when it comes to birds, so make sure you visit one that is familiar with bird diseases and ailments.

Pneumonia

Pneumonia often develops as a result of a prolonged cold or if a bird has withstood too much heat or too much cold. A great deal of excess fluid builds up in the bird's lungs, causing them to become very spongy as well as watery.

If a young bird catches pneumonia, it can usually recover but it will always remain frail and susceptible to various diseases throughout its life.

Treatment for this ailment is similar to that for a cold. However, it is essential to administer an antibiotic. Aureomycin, terramycin or achromycin is recommended.

If your macaw is extremely ill, it may be impossible to administer medication orally. Consult your veterinarian, as medication may have to be given through injection.

Psittacosis

Psittacosis, though a rarity, has caused a public uproar in past years because it is transmissible to humans. It is commonly known as "parrot fever." However, with the help of modern medicine, this disease can be controlled. Symptoms are similar to a severe cold or pneumonia. Antibiotics, aureomycin, terramycin and achromycin are used to combat the bacteria (actually a rickettsia). It is sometimes necessary to take a blood sample to accurately diagnose psittacosis.

Chances of your macaw contracting this bacteria are very slim. However, if you have sufficient reason to suspect that your bird is indeed afflicted with the disease, it would be best to have a blood test taken. Because a macaw is a large bird, the test should not prove harmful to him.

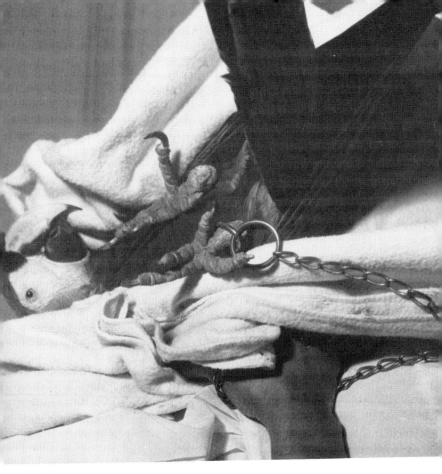

This is the proper way to hold a macaw, as a nervous bird can inflict a nasty wound with its beak or claws. It is also advisable to remove any chains to prevent the patient from breaking a leg.

Sinus Problems

Sinus trouble is a low-grade infection usually brought on by the aftermath of a cold. Probably the first symptom you will notice is small mounds on the bird's head or just above its eyes. These mounds are actually lumps of hardened mucus that have accumulated behind clogged sinus passages. The mounds are usually yellow and tend to have a cheese-like consistency. Other symptoms are swollen eyes (sometimes forced shut) and puffy sacs under the eyes.

The best way to relieve the bird is to first drain the mounds so as not to injure any tissue. Proper drainage should actually be done with minor surgery, pricking the mound with a sterilized pin. In a few days a scab will form. Massage the scab slightly to remove it. Do the best you can to remove all the cheese-like material so that the condition will not recur. Then cleanse the area with a mild disinfectant.

In order to clear swollen eyes and eye sacs, gently apply yellow oxide of mercury ointment for three or four days.

Asthma

Asthma is also brought on by the aftermath of a cold. Though it is a low grade infection, it may have to be treated for up to six months. If your bird has just recuperated from a cold but continues to have trouble breathing and makes a pathetic wheezing sound, it probably has asthma.

The best way to combat this ailment is to isolate the bird and administer an inhalent every day for an hour. Though this may seem like a slow way to cure the infection, it has to my knowledge the best results. Antibiotics have proved ineffective for treatment of asthma.

Diarrhea

Diarrhea, as previously mentioned, is actually a symptom of other disorders and it may also be caused by a change of diet. Diarrhea can be fatal if left unattended.

Certain medicines are prescribed for treatment, but some may be too harsh. I personally recommend Kaopectate® , which can be given every three hours. If your bird has bloody diarrhea *do not* administer any type of medicine, as it will only worsen the problem. In such a case it is best to call upon a veterinarian, as the type of treatment depends upon the cause.

Constipation

Constipation is usually caused by the presence of worms or mites in the bird's system or colds. When a bird is constipated, its droppings will be white.

You can clear the digestive tract and eliminate the trouble by administering the proper laxative. An oily laxative is most helpful in most cases.

Nausea

Macaws will regurgitate for several reasons. It usually means they have a desire to mate. They will purposely bring up their food to offer their mate. If a bird lives alone it might bestow this customary honor upon you. Try not to be discouraged or alarmed, for its odd behavior will pass quickly enough.

However, if the bird continues to vomit, it may be a sign of some disorder. Nausea is often associated with crop ailments including sour crop, crop impaction and molds. These maladies can be treated with antibiotics.

Going-Light

Going-light refers to loss of weight. It is actually a symptom rather than a disease. Going-light occurs when a bird has a high metabolic rate and needs to constantly make up for spent energy. When a parrot isn't feeling well it often goes off its diet, using its flesh for nourishment as a result. This, of course, can lead to rapid weight loss. This condition can also be fatal if the cause of the trouble is not found and treated.

Molds

Fungi are responsible for a great many illnesses in pet birds. Fungus molds can be contracted in numerous ways. Dirty water, rotten seeds, moldy food, dampness and filth all cause molds. Treatment varies depending on the type and location of the infection. Unfortunately, most treatments are unsuccessful. The best way to combat the problem is to prevent it altogether. Clean and disinfect the bird's living quarters frequently!

If your bird does develop a mold, it can affect many different parts of its body. Symptoms that resemble those of a cold are caused by molds in the mouth. Others affect the digestive tract and cause diarrhea. Some molds draw water from the bird, causing the bird's body to actually become mushy.

Copper sulfate is one remedy that often has the best results in treating molds if administered in diluted form. If your bird has an external mold, keep him in a warm room and clean the infected area with a mild disinfectant. Then apply a mild astringent.

Bacterial and Protozoan Enteritis

Enteritis is a deadly disease often contracted by aviary birds. It is caused by overcrowded and dirty living quarters. I must again stress the importance of cleanliness. A macaw living in filth is doomed. Your charges ask so little of you and give so much in return, they shouldn't have to suffer needlessly.

Symptoms of enteritis are diarrhea, weight loss, weakness and listlessness. The disease spreads quickly and can cause rapid death. Treat with aureomycin.

French Molt

Though macaws naturally molt (lose and grow new feathers) twice a year, continued feather loss and replacement is unhealthy. Birds with French molt are weak because the constant replacement of feathers takes all their strength. Most often birds suffering from this ailment look ruffled and are unable to fly.

Though the actual cause of French molt is unknown, many attribute it to either dietary deficiencies or mites. The best prevention is to spray your bird frequently to protect against mites and make sure you are feeding a well rounded diet.

Feather Plucking

Birds pull their feathers out because they are frustrated or because they are suffering from a dietary deficiency. If your bird lives in an environment rich with stimuli and you pay a good deal of attention to him, chances are something is lacking in his diet. You can remedy the situation by adding a dietary supplement (liquid vitamins are recommended) to its diet. See the chapter on feeding for further discussion of proper diet.

If your bird eats well, then perhaps it is bored. You can break its feather plucking habit by paying more attention to it and buying it more toys so that it can amuse itself while you're away.

Mites

Red mites are most common in aviary birds. They seem to attack hens and nestlings most often and actually suck their blood. If the aviary is heavily infested with red mites, they can cause the deaths of their victims. Inspect for mites in corners, cracks and behind nest boxes. These tiny pests are difficult to get rid of. The best solution is to spray cages once a week.

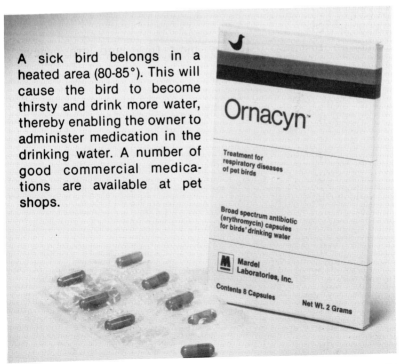

A sick bird belongs in a heated area (80-85°). This will cause the bird to become thirsty and drink more water, thereby enabling the owner to administer medication in the drinking water. A number of good commercial medications are available at pet shops.

Keep an eye out for scaly leg mites; they can cause the bird's legs to become inflamed. Normal preening, as being performed here, helps to eradicate some parasites.

Feather and quill mites can destroy a bird's plumage. If feathers appear ratty and chewed up there is good reason to suspect feather mites as the cause. Spray your bird or birds with a mild insecticide.

Scaly leg mites attack the bird's legs, often causing inflammation. You can treat your pet by applying mite-oil or salve directly on the infected areas. This should suffocate the mites and soothe inflammation.

Overgrown Beak and Claws

The beak and claws of a macaw grow in much the same way as our fingernails, at a fairly regular rate. Overgrowth can be attributed to a lack of material to chew on and perches that are too small to allow the bird to use its claws sufficiently.

If a beak becomes overgrown, it will have to be trimmed. This is not going to be an easy task with a macaw as you will have difficulty restraining it. It would be best if you had a partner to help you, then one of your could hold the bird while the other proceeds to trim its beak. A dog toe nail clipper will be the best tool for this task.

If you should accidently cut the vein in the beak, apply iron sulfate or hydrogen peroxide to stop the bleeding.

You can wear down overgrown claws by applying sand to the bottom of a perch (select a larger perch than the bird has been using) by painting it on with shellac.

Overgrown claws and beaks are obviously due to neglect. Please take precautions in the future so that they won't recur.

Egg-binding

Egg-binding can be a very serious condition if not detected and treated right away. It occurs when an egg gets caught in the oviduct. Occasionally female birds that are not

Allowing your macaw to chew on willow and fruit tree branches will prevent the overgrowth of the beak. Chewing is the most natural way to keep the beak trimmed and healthy. Beak-trimming conditioners are available at pet shops.

used for breeding lay eggs, therefore they can also be afflicted. Symptoms are ruffled feathers, loss of spirit, obvious weakness and straining gestures to remove the egg.

Treat the bird by placing it in a warm environment. The temperature should range between 80 and 85°F. Administer a bit of olive oil to the vent and massage the area very gently. Normally the egg will be laid within the next few hours.

Lack of proper diet and exercise causes egg-binding, which--as you should realize by now--can easily be avoided.

Tumors

Old macaws are more likely to have tumors than younger birds. Lipomas are benign fatty tumors that can be removed by surgery. Consult a veterinarian with the knowledge and proper equipment for this type of operation. Lipomas are usually found on the chest and occasionally on the bird's wings. Tumors on the wings are very painful as they sometimes grow so large the bird can't fold its wing properly. These can also be removed with surgery.

Not all tumors are benign. Many are cancerous and cannot be cured. These are often internal and impossible to detect.

Arthritis

Arthritis is also seen in older parrots. Though no one is sure of its cause, many believe it is a result of improper diet. Unfortunately, once a bird is afflicted with arthritis there is no cure. Again adequate diet and exercise will save your pet from unnecessary suffering.

• • • •

The treatments I have described in this chapter for various ailments are not always successful. However, they are responsible for a high rate of recovery. The best medication for the pet bird is prevention. As you must now be aware, a good percentage of diseases and ailments are a direct result of neglect. If you are a responsible pet owner and care for your bird in the manner I have described throughout this book, chances are your pet will live a long and healthy life, barring unforeseen trouble.

8. MACAWS
THE LARGER MACAWS
HYACINTH MACAW

The hyacinth macaw, *Anodorhynchus hyacinthinus* (Latham), is the largest member of the entire parrot family. It is nearly three feet long, with a large and powerful black beak. The overall coloring of the hyacinth is a lustrous cobalt blue. Its wings and tail are an even deeper shade of the same color. This species has a bright yellow ring around its eyes and along the sides of the lower part of its beak.

The hyacinth is a native of central Brazil south of the Amazon River. It lives in the buriti palm tree, which can be found in swamps surrounding lakes and rivers. Less social than most other macaws, this species is usually only seen in pairs. On occasion they are encountered in groups of five that are probably family units.

The hyacinth nests in the hollows of tree trunks or sometimes in cliffs and the female lays three eggs. Little else is known of these magnificent beauties in their wild state.

In captivity these birds soon grow tame and are exceptionally affectionate, but owing to their enormous size they are not suitable pets for the average bird fancier. Also, because the hyacinth is rare it is one of the most expensive macaws to purchase. For that matter, they are seldom offered for sale.

For those who do choose to own a hyacinth, there are only two suitable living accommodations: a very large made-to-order iron cage or a strong aviary. Why all the precaution? The hyacinth can snap off the end of a broom as easily as if it were a match stick. That's 300 pounds of biting pressure per square inch! It should be easy to guess what this bird is capable of doing to an average cage! Hyacinths also like to gnaw on wood, which explains why they should be kept in an iron cage.

63

The hyacinth is very hardy, though awkward and clumsy due to its enormous size. Once while I was feeding graham crackers to a beautiful group of macaws at a nearby zoo, I soon discovered that the one and only hyacinth was having a terrible time getting the cracker to its mouth. All the other birds anxiously extended a beak or claw through the wire fencing to take my offering. The hyacinth wasn't able to fit its beak through an opening, so it carefully extended a large black claw, in which I placed the cracker. With the cracker in place, the bird was unable to bring its foot back into the cage and up to its mouth. We tried again and again with smaller pieces to no avail. The crackers continually dropped to the ground. I never saw a more pitifully frustrated bird in all my life! The poor thing was so disgusted it chased all the other birds away from me, thinking, I suppose, that if he couldn't have any neither would they.

Hyacinths will practically destroy their perches with their incessant gnawing, so remember to replace perches frequently. This may seem to be a bit of a bother, but keep in mind that gnawing is essential to keep the beak in good condition and to prevent its overgrowth. Also, one should supply the hyacinth with green bark, foliage and fresh branches daily for gnawing.

During the winter, the hyacinth should be provided with a shelter that is slightly heated.

The hyacinth was first bred in captivity in Illinois in 1971 by R.C. Small.

BLUE AND GOLD MACAW

The blue and gold macaw, *Ara ararauna* (Linnaeus), also known as the blue and yellow, is one of the larger macaws. The cock grows to a length of approximtely 34 inches; the hen is slightly smaller. The tail, wings, back and neck of the

Opposite:
The blue and gold macaw was first bred in France in 1818. Hybrids between the blue and gold and the red and yellow are known.

Comfortable in their surroundings, these blue and gold macaws still remain alert. Photo by San Diego Zoo.

Severe macaws are difficult to sex. Photo by Horst Mueller.

A military macaw preening a hyacinth. Mutual preening is commonplace for these birds. Photo by Sam Fehrenz.

blue and gold are a bright, almost turquoise, blue. Its forehead and crown are a greenish blue. Deep golden yellow dominates its undersides except for a bluish yellow on the underparts of its tail and a black collar just beneath its face. Its cheek patch is white lined with a trace of black feathers. Beak and feet are totally black. The eyes can be either bright or pale yellow. Plumage is similar in both sexes.

This species can be found in the jungles of Panama and Colombia as well as in parts of Brazil, Venezuela, Ecuador and Peru. This suggests that the blue and gold is more adaptable to various environments in comparison to other macaws that are only found in localized areas.

In the wild, the hen will usually lay two glossy white eggs and hatch them on her own. The young birds will emerge between 23-24 days, although in captivity incubation time is between 25 and 28 days. They will remain in the nest until they are three months old, by which time they will have attained their full plumage.

In captivity the blue and gold will often nest and hatch young, but it usually takes a long time. It may even take years to breed successfully as it may be difficult to match two birds that will nest. And though it may sound silly, even if you bought two macaws for breeding purposes, guaranteed mates, they could very well turn out to be of the same sex. It does happen.

For those of you who wish to try breeding this species, a large hollow tree trunk or an old barrel with a round opening should be provided as a nesting box for the hen. The box should be 40" long, 2' wide and 32" high. The entrance can be either 10" square or 10" in diameter. The floor of the nesting box should be slightly slanted toward the back so that the eggs won't roll out. Macaws should be provided with a nest box all year because they will want to roost there. Keep in mind, if you decide to breed, that even the gentlest macaw will be very protective at this time and might become nasty.

Blue and golds deserve the highest praise. They are said to be somewhat more intelligent and alert than other species. Definitely curious, these birds have a knack for getting into mischief. They are among the better talkers. Many bird handlers consider the blue and gold to be the gentlest and most trainable of the macaws. This species tends to become attached to one person or sex, usually shying away from strangers. Naturally affectionate, the blue and gold makes a devoted pet.

Macaws are not always friendly towards other birds, so it is quite risky to keep two unrelated species together, even in an open area like a yard or garden. Only by gradually exposing the birds to each other can the problem be dealt with.

Lear's macaw (opposite) closely resembles the hyacinth macaw (above), but it is somewhat smaller and lacks the luster of the feathers. Both birds are a beautiful shade of cobalt blue with yellow patches on the face. Photos by San Diego Zoo.

Blue and gold macaws, like all other macaws, should be housed in a strong aviary where the wood is protected from their gnawing. In the winter it is essential to house them indoors, but no artificial heat is needed.

Crossings of the blue and gold macaw include:

Blue and gold X green-winged

Blue and gold X scarlet

SCARLET MACAW

The scarlet macaw, *Ara macao* (Linnaeus), also referred to as the red and yellow, is probably one of the most breathtaking parrots you will ever see. It is a large bird growing to a length of approximately 36 inches, nearly half of which is a long tapering tail. The hen is similar but slightly smaller with a shorter, broader beak. The overall coloring of the scarlet is a deep radiant red. The wings are a bright yellow and blue. The rump is light blue. Its tail is a deep shade of blue mixed with red. The scarlet's cheek patch is flesh-colored, and the beak is whitish on the upper mandible and black on the lower mandible.

These beautiful creatures are found in southern Mexico, Central America and the northwestern sections of South America. They are most comfortable in light woodland rather than humid forests. Scarlet macaws are very sociable birds and are usually seen in pairs, family parties or flocks of up to thirty. There is a deep bond between pairs. They can be spotted in flocks, flying side by side, their wings nearly touching. The birds leave their roost during the day in search of food, which is found in treetops. Their diet consists of seeds, fruits, nuts and berries. When night falls they return home. Little is known of their breeding habits other than they nest in the hollows of trees.

In captivity the scarlet is one of the more popular macaws, not only because of its beautiful plumage, but also for the dedication it bestows on the one who cares for it. This bird has the ability to speak clearly and, surprisingly enough, it is less expensive than some of the other popular species.

The first breeding records for the scarlet macaw date from 1916 (Britain). It takes approximately 25 days for the eggs to hatch. The youngsters leave the nest after about three months.

Opposite:
The green winged macaw is less sociable than the other macaws and in the wild is seen only in pairs or small parties. Photo by San Diego Zoo.

The military macaw is relatively easy to tame and has moderate talking ability. Photo by Horst Mueller.

These 5-week-old blue and gold macaws will grow into fine healthy specimens with proper care. Photo by A.J. Mobbs.

The scarlet has perhaps one real drawback, an earth-shattering screech. As one disgruntled owner so poetically put it, "A scarlet can shatter glass from a mile away." There is one saving grace: macaws usually only scream at certain times of the day or when they are bored and frustrated. If you are prepared to give your bird the proper attention it deserves, you will undoubtedly be rewarded with a loving, affectionate pet.

Scarlet macaws love to bathe and have been observed to sit in a light rain slapping themselves and maneuvering their bodies so as to wet themselves all over, much like humans behave in the shower.

An extremely large nest box should be provided all year long because the scarlet macaw will like to roost in the nest box as well as use it for breeding purposes. It would be wise to protect the corners from the gnawing of the birds by reinforcing them with metal strips.

There are a few known crossings of the scarlet macaw which include:

Scarlet X military.

Scarlet X blue and gold.

Scarlet X green winged.

GREEN WINGED MACAW

The green winged macaw, *Ara chloroptera* G.R. Gray, has a number of other names that often lead to confusion: red and blue macaw, red and green macaw, crimson macaw and the maroon macaw. Try to keep in mind if you come across these names that they are all referring to the same bird.

The plumage of the green winged is very similar to the scarlet with these exceptions: it is a deeper shade of red and the wings are dark green and blue instead of yellow and blue. The cheek patch is whitish with a trace of red feathers lining the face. The tail, which is shorter than the scarlet's, is blue splashed with deep red. The beak is horn white on the upper

The green winged macaw is one of the most expensive species. Hybrids with other types of macaws occur on a regular basis.

The green winged macaw is easily frightened by sudden movements and noises. Photo by Ray Hanson.

Illiger's macaw (right) adjusts very well to captivity. Photo by Horst Mueller.

The hyacinth macaw is a hardy bird but sometimes appears rather awkward and clumsy because of its immense size. Photo by Horst Mueller.

mandible, with the lower mandible black. The green winged has a large head and beak and a very stocky body. It grows to be approximately 32" long.

This macaw is most often found in the hilly country of eastern Panama and in many areas of South America. Like the scarlet, the green winged is seldom seen along the coast. It prefers the forests of the interior.

This species is very much like the other large macaws except that they usually travel in pairs or small parties not in flocks. During the nesting season, green wings live in pairs. The hen usually lays two eggs, sometimes three. The young hatch in 24-26 days. They leave the nest at three months, at which time they resemble the parents except that they have shorter tails.

This species is no longer readily available and therefore they are very expensive. However, their temperament is much like that of the hyacinth. They get along very well with children and pets. The green winged macaw has been bred successfully in captivity. They have proved to be excellent parents.

The green winged macaw is easily frightened by sudden movements and noises, therefore it is advisable to keep them in a fairly quiet environment. Remember that it is the instinctive reaction of a frightened macaw to bite.

This macaw was first bred in England in 1962 by J.S. Riff. From 1962-1968, they bred almost annually so that by 1968 he had reared 13 young.

MILITARY MACAW

The military macaw or great green macaw, *Ara militaris militaris* (Linnaeus), grows to a length of approximately 27"; the hen is slightly smaller. This bird is an overall olive green color. It has a deep red forehead, black beak, bluish red primary feathers and a tail that is olive yellow on the under surface and brownish red on the upper surface. The cheek patch is whitish with rows of violet brown feathers.

In the wild, the military macaw usually roosts in tree trunks or other nesting places. Military macaws should always be provided with branches to chew on or they are known to become very destructive.

The blue and gold and the scarlet macaws are two of the more popular species. Photo by Paradise Park, Hawaii.

Opposite:
The severe macaw is one of the most popular and most frequently available of the dwarf macaws. Photo by San Diego Zoo.

The military is easily tamed and has moderate talking ability. However, due to its comparatively dull coloring it has never gained the same popularity as the macaws previously mentioned. Some authorities feel that the military's personality is not quite up to par with the other species. For these reasons the military macaw is relatively inexpensive.

The military macaw is found in Mexico, the northwestern part of tropical South America and the tropical parts of Bolivia to the Argentine border. These birds are happiest in dry forests and open woodland, and they try to avoid tropical rainforests. They usually travel in pairs or in flocks of up to twenty. This is quite different from some other macaws who only live in pairs. Their habits are similar to the scarlet macaw's. They leave their roost in the early morning in search of food and return home at night. Their diet consists of seeds, nuts, berries, fruits and vegetable matter. When resting, they perch on the tops of very tall trees.

DWARF MACAWS

SEVERE MACAW

The severe macaw, *Ara severa severa* (Linnaeus), is one of the most popular of the dwarf macaws. It is also one of the most frequently available. The plumage of the severe greatly resembles that of the military macaw; however, this energetic little creature only grows to a length of approximately 20 inches.

The severe macaw is almost entirely dark green. Its crown is blue and its forehead deep brown at the base of the upper mandible. Its bare white cheek patch has a small trace of feathers. The flight feathers and upper side of the tail are blue mixed with green. Underwing coverts are red. The under side of the severe's tail is red mixed with brown. Beak and feet are black. The proportions of this species are much more appealing than that of the military macaw.

The severe macaw's natural habitat ranges from eastern Panama to the Guianas, south to northern Bolivia and in southern Brazil. They are seen frequently in tropical forest zones. The natural call of these parrots is higher pitched than the larger macaws. Their cries also seem to have a complaining ring.

The severe nests high up in the hollows of dead trees. The hen usually lays a single egg. In captivity severes make loving and affectionate pets. They possess all of the charm of their cousins but are somewhat easier to accommodate due to their smaller size. They can live contentedly in a large cage but should be allowed out for extra exercise.

It is difficult to select a pair of severes for mating purposes, just as it is with most other species, due to the similarity of plumage between the sexes. However, if you do buy a mated pair, they can be kept in a small sturdy aviary and should be able to breed. A nesting box for this species should be 16 inches high, 16 inches wide and have a 16-inch circular entrance. Damp soil and a little moss should be placed on the bottom of the box to allow for sufficient moisture to keep the eggs from becoming too dry. You can expect to find two or three eggs that should hatch in approximately 28 days. The young will remain in the nest for about seven weeks after fledging and will still be fed by the parents.

Since the severe is a dwarf macaw it, along with the other dwarf macaws, has some special food requirements. They should be fed canary seed, millet, hemp and some greens and branches.

The severe macaw is quite sensitive to cold and drafts, therefore it is advisable to winter them inside with some artificial heat.

The blue and gold is one of the more popular macaws. It is one of the most brilliantly colored and probably the best talker. Photo by Hawaiian Service Slides.

Opposite:
The yellow-naped macaw is famous for its comedic behavior. Photo by San Diego Zoo.

ILLIGER'S MACAW

The Illiger's macaw, *Ara maracana* (Vieillot), is somewhat similar to the severe, but it only grows to a length of 17 inches. The overall coloring is an olive green. Its forehead is orange red followed by a bluish green head. The Illiger's has a red patch on its belly and lower back. Wings are blue and green. The tail is blue. Its eyes are a reddish brown, the cheek patch and cere are yellow. Its beak is blackish brown and its legs are flesh-colored. The hen is basically the same in coloring except that the red on its forehead is duller.

Illiger's macaw is a native of eastern Brazil and northeastern Argentina. It is a bird of the forest, found particularly in areas near waterways. It is usually seen in pairs or small parties. Unlike other miniature macaws, this bird has a distinctive flight pattern. It does not fly straight and true, but rather jerks up in flight in a bucking motion. Its natural call is a deep guttural screech.

This species adjusts very well to captivity. They quickly become tame and are extremely affectionate. Unlike some other birds, they love to be petted. However, they have a tendency to be moody and occasionally they lose their temper and snap. Otherwise, they make fine pets.

The Illiger's macaw needs a nest box of approximately 15"x15" in order to have any chance of breeding. They will also use this nest box all year round to roost in. In the opinion of Dr. M. Vriends, breeding successes are greatly improved if they are fed all year on bits of bread soaked in milk. The young in the nest should be fed on a high protein diet.

YELLOW-NAPED MACAW

The yellow-naped macaw, *Ara auricollis* (Cassin), also referred to as the yellow-collared, is another member of the green dwarf macaws. This species grows to a length of about 16-18 inches. It is basically dark green with a black forehead and an attractive yellow collar on the back of its neck. The primary and secondary feathers, along with the tail feathers, are splashed with blue. The cheek patch is white. The eyes are reddish and its beak is black.

The yellow-naped macaw is a native of eastern Bolivia, Paraguay, several areas of Argentina and some parts of Brazil. They are plentiful in swamplands and are seen most frequently in flocks. In captivity the yellow-naped has a sharp, high pitched screech. Little is known of their natural call or habits in the wild.

They make excellent pets and are known for their endearing and clownish behavior, especially in the morning. This species, along with the other dwarfs, is considerably less expensive than the larger macaws. This makes them attractive to the bird fancier who can't afford to purchase a large macaw but is intrigued by the personalities of these magnificent parrots.

RED-BELLIED MACAW

The name of this miniature macaw, *Ara manilata* (Boddaert), red bellied, is very misleading as the bird only has a faint trace of red on its belly. If anything, this bird should rightly be called the black headed macaw. Basically green, the red-bellied macaw's forehead is black, followed by bluish green on the nape of its neck. Primary flight feathers are blue with black tips. The tail has a dull reddish tinge on the upper side and a light yellow tinge on the under side. Its beak is dark but lighter at the tips.

It is a native of southeastern Venezuela and northeastern Peru and Brazil. They are typically found in palm swamps and usually live in pairs or small groups. These macaws like to rest during the day and then become active around four o'clock in the afternoon. They are not very sociable but occasionally associate with orange-winged amazons. Little else is known of their habits in the wild. They are quite rare and seen very infrequently in captivity. This species was imported into Europe in 1872 (Amsterdam Zoo "Artis"). There is no record of the species having bred in captivity.

A blue and gold macaw "answers" the phone in Paradise Park, Hawaii. These large macaws are among the most intelligent of the macaws. Photo by Dr. Herbert R. Axelrod.

Opposite:
The noble macaw is the smallest macaw, measuring only 12 inches at maturity. Photo by San Diego Zoo.

NOBLE MACAW

This adorable little creature, *Ara nobilis cumanensis* (Lichtenstein), is the smallest of all macaws, growing to a length of only twelve inches. It is sometimes confused with the blue crowned conure. Its one identifying marking is its bare cheek patch.

The noble macaw is an overall dull green. Its underwings are red, the flight feathers splashed with black. Its beak is also black. The crown and forehead of the noble macaw are bluish, and its five-inch tail is tinged with yellow.

These petite macaws are found in the Guianas, eastern Venezuela and southern Brazil. They are generally encountered in flocks that are easily detected as they are very noisy birds and screech loudly while in flight. In captivity, these birds easily become tame and are very gentle. They make lovely pets and are famous for their mimicry. Mrs. von Proschek (Vienna) had a male that could speak over 50 words.

The birds are available on the American and European market from time to time, but the first record of breeding in captivity dates from 1949 (Vane, England). The noble macaw was first exhibited in Berlin in 1879.

Opposite:
ame macaws are delightful playmates and will be fine,
rustworthy pets provided they are well cared for. However,
ou should never tease these birds, as they are rather un-
redictable regardless of tameness or age. With the proper
are and attention, they make the finest pets.

Blue and gold macaw.
Opposite:
Hyacinth macaw

Index